T0146514

JEWELS TOO...
The Journey Continues

DANETTE M. REID

authorHOUSE®

AuthorHouse™
1663 Liberty Drive
Bloomington, IN 47403
www.authorhouse.com
Phone: 1 (800) 839-8640

Published by AuthorHouse   05/16/2016

ISBN: 978-1-5246-0856-9 (sc)
ISBN: 978-1-5246-0855-2 (e)

Library of Congress Control Number: 2016907997

Print information available on the last page.

CONTENTS

DEDICATION

This book is dedicated to my three heartbeats: George, Danae, and George, III. I love each of you with an everlasting love.

A NOTE OF THANKS

Seven is the biblical number of completion and the exact number of years between my first and second book. Thank you God for allowing me to continue to travel along this journey. Your presence and guidance in my life has been nothing short of amazing. The path hasn't always been easy but you continue to honor Your Word and I am a grateful servant. Thank you for choosing me to encourage and uplift others. Thank you for my husband, George, my children, Danae' and George, my parents, Patricia and James Eastland and my sisters, Chariesse Eastland and Charlene Cruz. Thank you for my sister circle, Angie Dennis, Erica Martin, Yvette Styer, Robyn Tucker, Roslyn McLaurin, Kristen Cuthbert, Alleronda Harris, Autumn Redcross, and Sarita Brooker. Thank you for my amazing team members, Sonia Clough and Renee Raysor-Winstead. Thank you for my in-loves especially Joan Reid, Kimberly Reid, Scott Reid, Judy Trusty and Lisa Trusty. Thank you for my amazing Sorors of Delta Sigma Theta Sorority, Inc. Thank you for my adopted sons and daughters that have welcomed me into their villages. Thank you for my nieces and nephews. Thank you for enlarging my territory and surrounding me with light and love.

I love you beyond words.

INTRODUCTION

To find your authenticity, you must become transparent with yourself. You must look in the mirror and own your truth. Do not be afraid of the journey because God will be with you every step of the way. Welcome to my truth!

If anyone would have told me that one day I would be the author of two books, I would have looked around to make sure that they were speaking to me! By trade, I am a small business owner working in the insurance industry. Writing was not on my radar. But God in His infinite wisdom gave me a gift, took me through the valley to hone it, and placed a spirit of encouragement in my heart. He showed me my purpose and I have been following Him to the best of my ability since He revealed my gift to me. When I first released Jewels from My Journey, I had no idea whether I would even sell one book. I wasn't doubtful, just unsure if I heard Him right. Jewels Too has been in the works for quite some time but again in His time, He gave me the vision and set the plan in motion for it to reach the people that He needs it to reach. If you are reading this, then you are one of those people.

It is my prayer that something you read will move you, make you laugh, and perhaps shed a tear or two as you realize that God has you covered!

CHAPTER 1

Peaceful Living

Peace I leave with you; my peace I give you. I do not give to you as the world gives. Do not let your hearts be troubled and do not be afraid. John 14:27

An early morning walk and a post refocused me! I became Martha (business) when I wasn't paying attention. I became busy in the kingdom but stopped focusing on my true purpose and relationship with God in an effort to be there for the church. It is hard but I'm stepping away from some things outside of my purpose so that I can get back to the basics. Bible Study. Daily and fervent prayer. Meditation. Daily conversations with God. This is what I will be focusing on... I am in search of a deeper relationship, I am moving to a better me.

The Intersection

*The Lord gives strength to his people; the Lord blesses his people with peace.
Psa 29:11*

One day, while traveling along this journey, I met a girl named Drama.
We became fast friends. She was a great listener and I told her all about
my family and friends. She was a private person and didn't share much
about her home life with me. I spent all of my time with her and before
long, she placed me at odds with just about everyone I knew. After several
uncomfortable encounters arranged by Drama, I sadly realized that she was
someone who specialized in confusion and disarray. Soon, being around
her was no longer fun. Much to Drama's dismay, I ended our friendship.
Her parting words to me that day were "if you ever need me, I live on But
Street."

A few months following the end of our friendship, I was bored and decided
to locate Drama. The only information that I had was that she lived on But
Street. I grabbed my keys and headed out to reunite with my old friend. I
entered But Street into my GPS and found that she lived in a little town
called Decision. According to the directions, her street is near a yield sign
and intersects with So Street.

When I arrived in Decision, I noticed that several roads would lead me to
Drama's home. My GPS went on the blink forcing me to stop at the nearest
gas station to ask for directions. The cashier mentioned that I could take
any of the roads because they all led to Drama but the ones that would
lead me there quickly were:

- I probably shouldn't tell you this But girl, did you know...
- I know I shouldn't lie about this, But if I tell the truth then she'll know I started it...
- I know I should not do this, But...
- I promised her that I wouldn't tell her business, But I have to tell someone. Promise me you won't breathe a word ....

I thanked the nice gentleman and turned to leave. I was really excited. I had found the way back to my old friend. As I was leaving, the cashier said, "Miss, But Street is a very busy street. You will have to yield to the other traffic. I always recommend that people take So Street instead. So Street is much nicer. However, if you decide to continue onto But Street, you won't be able to miss Drama's house. It's the biggest house in our town."

Well, that day, I never made it to Drama's house. Just as the cashier stated, But Street was really crowded. I decided to take his advice and instead of waiting, I turned onto So Street. He was correct. So Street was much nicer. I parked my car and was about to walk around the corner to find Drama until I met Peace. She was friendly and kind. We struck up a conversation and she told me that sometimes she gets lonely because the road to her house is much less traveled. She was really nice. I didn't understand why her friends were few. She believed that her lack of friends was due to the fact that she was quiet and still so perhaps, folk found her boring. She is faithful and loyal yet she's often overlooked because Drama is loud, loves attention, and appears to have more fun. I promised her that day that I would be back to visit often. As day grew into night, I prepared to leave. Before I left, I asked her if there was a shorter distance to travel when I returned the next time so that I could avoid those traveling to see Drama.

To my surprise, she said that I would find her by using the same streets that I used to find Drama. My wise friend smiled and said "In the town of Decision, everyone arrives at the intersection of "But," and "So." For instance if you travel the "I promised her that I wouldn't tell her business… you will come to the crossroad which has a yield sign. At that point, you must decide whether to travel along the road of **But** I have to tell someone or **So** I won't. The choice is yours. If you choose **But**, you will find Drama and if you choose So, you will find me. Again the choice is yours."

We bid farewell and I returned home. From that point forward, I have chosen "Peace." Now it's your turn to decide….

Mark 4:39 And he arose, and rebuked the wind, and said unto the sea, Peace, be still. And the wind ceased, and there was a great calm.

Natural Beauty

There's something unique about nature that brings me peace. I don't consider myself to be a person who loves the outdoors. Yet the sound of a water fall or finding a tree log that is out of place always brings a smile to my face. Maybe I love it because it gives me a chance to escape the thoughts that swirl in my head. You know, the thoughts that many of us have on occasion. Thoughts like "Am I doing it right," "What is life," "Is there more that I should be doing, and "Why does happy sometimes betray me and give way to pain." Or perhaps it is the pure serenity of personally experiencing the scripture "peace be still" where everything has its place and there is order and balance. It is in this space that I truly feel that it is effortless to be one with my Creator. I hear His voice in the rustling of the leaves. I see Him smile at me through a rock that causes the water to ripple. I look at a branch and visit my childhood of yesterday. I look at the sky and see a bright future. There are no worries or sorrows in this place and stress knows that she is defeated when I am here. I need to find more time to enjoy these moments for it is here where my spirit is free and grateful. It is here where peace expresses itself to me in its totality. No one could offer the gift of this beauty except God Himself. Thank you God for thinking so much of me that you would offer me the best though I am undeserving. Peace. Yes, I love the sound of that!

Beautiful Day

The birds are chirping and my husband is gently nudging me in the back. This is his way of signaling that I am snoring too loud. An hour later, my son runs upstairs to announce that he doesn't need an alarm clock today; he's already up, dressed, and ready to go. My daughter is clearly irritated because her brother is making too much noise. She walks into the bathroom grumbling about life not being fair as most teenagers her age do each morning. After our normal morning ritual, we load the car and get on the road. It's a new day and we are heading to the Philadelphia International Airport to begin a weeklong vacation in Hawaii. I can feel the stress leaving my body as we board the plane. My goal is to catch up on some much needed rest. Sleep does not find me; relaxation decides to visit instead. I adjust my iPod and let my mind be filled with the music of my favorite singer, India Arie. She is singing "Beautiful Day" and her words remind me that life is a journey comprised of seconds which become hours which become days which become months which become years. In twenty-four hours, this day will vanish and become yesterday. As I continue listening to this amazing songstress, I think about the fact that in fifteen hours, I will have traveled through several time zones to reach my destination. I will actually be six hours behind where I am at this very moment. Something about that thought makes me both teary-eyed and humbled.

I am humbled by the fact that the God that loves me is in both my past, present, and future. When I move forward, He is there. When I think back, He was there. When I consider this very moment, the one we call present, He is here with me. I am teary-eyed due to my gratitude. I have been blessed to experience a new day. It is a gift that God has unwrapped for me. It is one that will not come this way again and I am blessed each and every time I get to experience another piece of time. No two days are exactly the same. Some days are filled with great joy while others may offer great challenge. Some are simple and dare I say, forgettable, while others hold memories that I will treasure for a lifetime. Regardless of the day and what it brings, a new day is not guaranteed. So, while I have breath, I will always remember to offer thanks to God, our Father for His new mercy and grace. I will start my day with thanks and allow the same God who kept me yesterday to guide me today, tomorrow and always.

This for me is the beginning of Peace. Thank you, Ms. India for the reminder that today indeed is a Beautiful Day.

Year End

I am not big on resolutions. Instead, I prefer to reflect on the year that I am about to leave behind. This ritual has been cleansing for my soul. As I continue on this journey, I have come to understand that with the passing of time, we both lose and gain. We lose a moment, but if used wisely, we gain experience, wisdom, and a memory. The impact of the lessons I have learned along the way have continued to shape and refine me. Since I began this ritual, I have gained the following:

2000 – Don't allow the issues of this world and all the hype that comes with it make you lose sight of the fact that God, the Father, Son, and Holy Spirit are in charge of the what, who, how, and when in your life.

2001 - Stepping out on faith is not just a cliché. It is real. December 1, 2001, the doors of the Danette M. Reid State Farm Agency went from a dream to reality.

2002 – Family first means sacrifice and prioritizing and for that I will offer no apology.

2003 – God will send you reminders and correction when you veer off course. You have two choices. Fight it or accept it. I choose to accept it and have been made better for it.

2004 – God is in control and will provide you with what you need to continue along your path.

2005 – Sometimes the best decisions are also the toughest ones to make but are necessary for growth, opportunity, and peace of mind.

2006 – In the blink of an eye, a loved one can be called home. Do not assume that you have tomorrow to get things right with one another. If you love someone, tell them and then tell them again.

2007 – What the enemy means to bring you harm; God will use for your good. God breathed life into Midweek Motivation… during a dark time in my life. Thank you Jesus!

2008 – Stay hopeful, on task, and watch God do what others thought to be impossible!

2009 – Trust in Him to see you through. He was, is, and forever will be. He is the first and the last. Put not your trust in man but in all your ways acknowledge Him and ask Him to direct your path.

2010 – When you walk in your purpose, even the detours along the way will work for your good.

2011 – As long as I have breath, it is not too late to follow my dream. Twenty-one years after my college graduation, I have returned to continue my education.

2012 – In a world filled with chaos and discontent, it is important to surround yourself with people who help you find your smile.

2013 – You have to give people room to grow. Everyone may not arrive at the same time but that doesn't mean that they won't show up. Intercessory prayer is a powerful tool.

2014 – One of the hardest things one ever has to do is to decide when the rubber meets the road in their life. You know, the part where you decide to live authentically as your best self without apology. Someone won't be happy with your newfound freedom. Make sure that somebody isn't you.

2015 – I've never met a person who became successful by focusing on what they could not do. Focus on the possibility. Focus on what can be done. Focus on the gift. The rest will fall in place. Success is in your reach.

Coffee Run

My husband loves coffee. His day starts and ends with a trip to the local Dunkin Donuts®. Family and friends alike often comment that we need to purchase stock in the company. His order is always the same: medium coffee with extra cream and extra sugar. The cashiers smile when they see him coming because he's a regular. They know him by name and when he steps up to the counter, his coffee is already prepared.

My husband's coffee experience is similar to my prayer life. I go to God daily and I believe He smiles when He sees His daughter coming. He knows what I am going to ask for before words are uttered from my lips. He knows that I am going to thank Him for a new day and share my concerns. He knows that I am going to talk to Him about my husband, children, and family. He knows everything that will take place and has actually already prepared the space for me to share. I enjoy our time together. It is time that is special and free of distraction. I find strength, peace, and a sense of belonging in our time together.

At one point in my life, I was inconsistent with my prayer life. I would pray based on my needs, feelings, and the situations I was facing. If I was experiencing a rough period, challenge, or uncomfortable situation, I would stop praying as often. There were even times, when I didn't pray at all due to my immature reaction to life's setbacks. It was during those times that I thought God had forgotten me. Not seeking Him was my payback for the perceived non-response. As I grew in faith and deepened my relationship with Him, I realized how backward my thinking had been. Instead of pulling away during times of uncertainty, those were the times I should have been pressing into Him more.

Thankfully, time has brought wisdom into my life and not a day goes by where He doesn't hear from me. Let today be a reminder that He has not forgotten you and I implore you not to forget about Him. Keep Him first in your life and talk to Him every day!

Vacation Time

If Puerto Rico was a person, this is what I'd tell her: from the trek through the rainforest to the walking tour of Old San Juan to the Go-kart race at the bottom of the mountain and so much more, this has indeed been a great vacation. I found out that iguanas like pizza and blueberry muffins but they don't like oranges. The birds and turtles however enjoyed the citrus fruit immensely. We spent the morning feeding them from a distance though I'm pretty sure we weren't supposed to do so. Every day was amazing yet profoundly filled with simplicity. Puerto Rico, I'd like to offer you a toast. Here's to Danaé finding a coconut as it washed ashore and us dreaming of making our own coconut oil empire. To running inside the hotel just because. To Danae's first trip at a casino with Skip. She was up to $16 and left with less than a dollar. To Tre and Skip trying Mufongo while I just sampled. To me trying Sangria and deciding that I am indeed a non-drinker. We didn't even finish the overpriced drinks. He ordered a Long Island ice tea with the same result. To Tre staking the umbrella on the beach only to have it blow away with the first wind. To getting caught with natural hair in the rain. To having never heard of yucca sticks before to opting for and enjoying them with ketchup instead of fries. To not being afraid to grab a map, ok really it was Siri™, and hit the road to discover unknown places. To finding a Krispy Kreme and navigating traffic to get to that side of the road. To jumping in the ocean and letting the waves take over. To watching the kids dig in the sand until they reached the water and then requesting that I stick my feet down there. To me hesitantly sticking my feet in the hole and surprisingly enjoying the free mud bath. To sitting in total silence and listening to the morning song of the birds. To life. To love. To peace. Until next time Puerto Rico, thanks for the memories! Cheers!

Diamond Peace

Have you ever experienced an "ah-ha" moment? You know, the ones that are life changing and bring you an incredible amount of peace and stillness. I'm not sure about you, but my "ah-ha" moments aren't always fun. In fact, more often than not, they seem to follow an intense experience where I've felt pressure, frustration, and uncertainty. During those times, I feel like I'm in a fog but something inside tells me to push through. What later emerges after the push through is what I lovingly refer to as a diamond peace. Diamond peace is peace that brings an invaluable lesson into my life. I began documenting my diamond peace years ago following an especially difficult period in my professional life. Over the years, I have collected the most diamond peace after taking an honest assessment of the lessons I've learned.

1. Just because you can does not mean that you should! Use your discernment wisely. God will never steer you wrong!
2. The art of appreciation will enter your life once you learn to thank God for what He's already provided.
3. With the dawn of each new day, we have an incredible opportunity to be kind to others.
4. Never allow anyone to place you where God has not instructed you to stand.
5. If you want to know something, ask, do not assume. False assumptions will lead to unintended outcomes.
6. You are responsible for you.
7. God. Family. Everything else. If this is not your current order, then you are out of order.
8. I measure success by the difference made, not the money earned.
9. Your blessing could be tied up in the way you respond to adversity. Before you get frustrated by a situation, remember: *And we know that all things work together for good to them that love God, to them who are called according to his purpose* (Rom 8:28).
10. Holding onto a moment of peace is worth far more than holding onto a grudge.

In the stillness of a quiet moment, peace can be found. Often we are so busy with life that we forget to just breathe and let it be.

My New Friend "Zippy"

I remember the day well. We were sitting at my sister's house discussing potential family outings. The conversation quickly turned to zip lining. Admittedly, I didn't think about the fact that in order to zip line would require climbing into trees and being carried through paths with a single cable. I enjoyed myself immensely and it's something that I can now place in my "done" column. As I thought back on that summer day, I imagined what the Zip Line, affectionately known as Zippy, would say to me if it could talk. I believe it would have gone something like this:

Danette, Danette, Danette! You are about to experience an adventure. I will be in charge and if you listen to the instructor, I will take you places you never dreamed of going. You will fly across the water, climb higher than you ever imagined, and realize that you can do things that you never thought possible. There's one key to this though and that is faith. You have to believe that I can carry you even when you think it's too hard to go on. You have to let go of your fears and learn to enjoy the exhilarating ride even if you don't yet know where you'll land. Be confident and know that if you stay connected, you will be just fine. You may get a few bumps and bruises along the way but that is par for the course and a reminder of how far you've come. So, on the count of three, let's do this! Enjoy the ride.

PS Tell the ones who read this to be encouraged and keep the faith. God is still in charge!

"When the two conflict, I will choose peace over popularity."

No Ordinary Day

Today started out as it always does. The kids are off to school, my husband has left for work, and I am on my way to the office. As I travel that very familiar road, the magnitude of a marquis I saw a few days ago interrupts my thoughts:

"Things that can be counted don't always count and things that count cannot always be counted. – Author Unknown"

In that instant, my regular schedule became secondary. It was replaced by a day spent mentally sorting through the list of things that I have accomplished in my recent past. My mind raced as I recalled the last few months. I thought about the times when I missed being home in time to watch the game with my son. I thought about the times when I said to my daughter that we would do it tomorrow and tomorrow still had not come. I thought about the last time I visited with my parents and in doing so, realized that I also had not been calling as much as I had in the past. I thought about times when I was on the phone or dabbling on social media when my husband wanted my attention. It was a scary thought but I had to accept that if it were a contest; the things, not the people were winning.

This was a painful lesson for me because prior to that jolt, I thought that I had become an expert at work life balance. The words on that marquis, however, forced me to evaluate and reconsider how my time was being spent. Later that day, I pulled out a sheet a paper and made a monthly checklist to serve as a daily reminder not to lose focus of what really matters. The sheet hangs in my closet and lists everything from regular visits to Delaware to see my parents, daily time for prayer and bible study to date nights with my husband and family game and movie nights. I have been doing a much better job thanks to that marquis and the list in my closet. I pray this is the last time I have to be reminded that things don't create memories; people do.

CHAPTER 2

Lost in My Thoughts

Sometimes, I get lost in my thoughts. Writing has helped me find my tears. Writing has captured my laughter. Writing has reminded me that each day serves as a piece of my story. Writing has given me the gift of knowing that my story is yet unfolding. As I move in and out of my thoughts, I offer you a glimpse.

Wish a World

If I had a million wishes, I'd only need a few. I'd wish for world peace. An end to hunger. An end to abuse. An end to poverty. An end to racism. An end to classism. An end to sexism. Then I'd give away the other wishes to those who would treat them as the gift that they were. They would build programs to provide economic equality. They would ensure quality education for all. They'd use them for all kinds of good and we would learn how to live together embracing our uniqueness without judging others for their own. Jealousy wouldn't exist and evil doing would have no place. I wish a world like this. I may never experience such a world, but that won't stop me from wishing it for future generations because the God we serve has filled me with hope and faith.

My tears

A tear slid down my cheek. It captured all that my words could not. It was filled with sadness for the senseless killings that are plaguing our communities. It was filled with frustration for the hatred that is so easily spewed between the races. It was filled with anger knowing that real change can only happen when we stop playing politics. It was filled with remembering the bright smile of a young man named Josiah who won his battle against cancer by becoming one of God's angels. It was filled with knowing that someone will go to bed hungry. It was filled with the thought that a child is being abused as I write this. It was a tear of despair. The second tear slid down right behind it. This tear held a different meaning. This one was filled with hope. It held onto the promise of a new day filled with grace and mercy. It was filled with gratitude that even though everything is not perfect, all is not lost. It was filled with the understanding that no matter what things look like, God is able to do abundantly above all that my mind is capable of conceiving. As the tears intertwined, my heart was filled and a reminder was given that now is not the time to turn away from my purpose. I must dig in, use my words, influence, and resources to do my part to change the world. And with that, I wiped my tears, repositioned my posture, put a smile on my face and went out to face the new day.

If the red light could talk...

What are you rushing for? When you see me, you need to STOP. I really wish you'd respect me instead of running through me as if I am not necessary. It's gotten so bad that cameras are now installed in certain areas to force you to STOP. Let me ask you a question. Is it that serious that you would risk getting pulled over and ticketed or worse yet, that you risk not only your life but others who may be in your path? The question then leads me to wonder if you act this way in other aspects of your life. Are you always on the go? Do you ignore the signs telling you to stop for a minute? Is your foot always on the pedal forging ahead nonstop? When do you rest? Is your schedule so full that taking a break is not an option? If these questions cause you to pause, then my advice to you is simple: Slow down. If you have every moment of every day planned then you aren't living. You are merely existing based on a to-do list. You need to take your foot off of the pedal and stop for a minute. Get some rest and refuel yourself physically, emotionally, and spiritually. Pray for clarity during your downtime. Take inventory. See what needs to be delegated or removed from your life so that you are able to carve out time for you on a regular basis. Trust me, when you STOP and get your rest, you will benefit in ways that I can't begin to explain. I hope you remember our talk once this light turns green! Only time will tell.

Afternoon drive

I was driving down a tree lined road today and was in awe of the picturesque beauty. While traveling, I considered the message of the trees. It was powerful and simple, yet the thought had never entered my head before that moment: The trees are all different. No two are exactly alike yet the beauty that lies in each one joins together and forms a sight to behold. If only we humans of different races, hues, backgrounds, etc. could embrace our uniqueness in such a manner, the result would be beautiful!

Gifts

The best gifts in life are often packaged differently than expected. While out looking for your gift, you may actually be overlooking the gifts that stare you in the face. Let me help you with a few examples. My husband is both younger and shorter than me, which by society's standards is not acceptable. Yet this man has been my rock, lover, and best friend for over twenty five years. We will soon celebrate twenty years of marriage and yes, we are still in love. I didn't like my best friend from High School when we first met and now she's been my sister for over thirty years. I was turned down for a job that I wanted only to realize that the career I have now allows me the freedom and flexibility to run a business and make myself available for my family, friends, and community at a moment's notice. I was introduced to my line sister through her mom who happened to knock on my door in college to see my room and have me meet her shy daughter. I have many more examples of gifts that I could share but I think you get the point. What God has for you will find you and they will be gifts that are far greater than anything you can buy. Today, I am grateful for my gifts.

Resistance

There was a time when the biggest obstacle to my quest for authenticity was resistance. I knew that finding my true self required dealing with my realities and some of those realities were things I'd like to avoid. In order to live authentically, I had to learn to accept that the person that I am is made up of both strengths and weaknesses. Dealing with my strengths has always been easy; it is the weaknesses that have challenged me for they reveal my shortcomings. Once upon a time, I convinced myself into believing that my weaknesses didn't deserve my attention. I was great at masking them and sometimes even pretended that they did not exist. In hindsight, I think I felt that if I didn't acknowledge that I needed to address certain areas of my life, then they would disappear. Growth has allowed me to see that resistance is an emotional obstacle that seeks to block authenticity. It allows you to wear a mask and become a great actor. I've toyed with resistance more than a few times in my life. Thankfully, I've come to know that uncovering and dealing with the real issue is far more important than pretending. Pretending wears off. Pretending holds me captive. Pretending gives power to the weaknesses. I'm no longer interested in playing that game. What I'm after is truth and authentic living. That is the destination that I seek and I am well on my way.

Sometimes you are in the way of what God desires for you. Stop driving and be His passenger. The place He is taking you is much further than you'd get by traveling alone.

Control Top Pantyhose

Dear Danette, you picked me up in the wrong size. I won't be a good fit for you. You will try every little trick you can think of but the result will be the same. I'm not a good fit. Though I hope you don't waste your time with me, I know you will. You see, you want to make it work if you can because you aren't a quitter. You want me to fit at any cost and maybe for a while I will. Eventually, you will understand and accept that if you try to make me fit, you will become uncomfortable because I wasn't meant for you. Don't say I didn't warn you and don't resent me for the time wasted. Just use it as a lesson that if it, whatever "it" happens to be, isn't meant for you, let it go so that you can be free to receive what God has in store for you.

Sincerely,
Queenie ☺

Friendship…What time has taught me

The essence of friendship is a sweet kiss from God above. It is found in the fun time spent together doing nothing at all. It fills a room with its loving presence. It is strengthened through the honest talks that help each other grow. It seeks not to offend and apologizes when it does. It is soothing when life throws curveballs. It challenges when it sees you standing in your own way. It holds your hand when a loved one passes or a relationship ends. It is honest and authentic. It doesn't always agree but knows how to disagree and remain in place. It rallies the troops when an intervention is needed. It is not threatened by another's presence because it is confident with the place it holds in your heart. It knows your character and defends it when someone attempts to defame it. It sticks by you through the lean times. It celebrates your accomplishments. It prays with you through your setbacks and failures. It doesn't keep tabs on the wrongs you've committed; it helps you deal with them and moves on. It doesn't judge you nor is it critical of your every move but it does "check" you when necessary. It walks in when others walk out. It can decipher the true meaning behind your cryptic text message. It wipes your tears, snot included. It sits on the phone with you until you are ready to talk. It shows up on your doorstep when you've told it to leave you alone. It knows when to push and when to stand by and let you find your own way. It is memorable and heartwarming. It is powerful and life changing. It is worth its weight in gold. It is indeed a blessing so once you have it, make sure you reciprocate it because the same person bringing friendship into your life deserves to receive it as well.

Love

Three little words strung together have the ability to ignite an internal explosion and awaken a hidden emotion. Do not withhold this sentence for the receiver is probably waiting to utter them as well. Simply put, "I love you" has incredible power but should only be used when he is willing to back it up with actions that let her know that she's his queen and he'd move mountains to keep her in his life...She in turn, will do the same. A love like this is rare so embrace it when it comes to greet you! Ignite it every day. Be the man that God has called you to be. Be the woman that God has called you to be. Together, you are one. Love like this has the power to restore families, overcome obstacles, and set an example for others to follow.

Chapter 3

Adversity

Jer 15:20-21 (NIV) I will make you a wall to this people, a fortified wall of bronze; they will fight against you but will not overcome you, for I am with you to rescue and save you, declares the Lord. I will save you from the hands of the wicked and redeem you from the grasp of the cruel.

When you think you've got nothing left to give, look inward and upward. The Spirit within is connected to the Father above and He didn't make you to be a quitter.

Failure

If my failure could talk, this is what she would say to me...

Hey you, can you hear me? I don't understand why you are smiling. This didn't work and now you have to switch gears. I know when you first realized that I won and you lost, you were sad and I think I even saw a tear form in your eye. I was pretty excited when you were distraught. But then something strange happened. You took a deep breath and thought back over other times when you didn't accomplish what you thought you would. Then, slowly the hunch in your back and the slouch of your shoulders straightened and the look of defeat was soon replaced with a smile. I heard you uttering something under your breath. You kept repeating it until it pierced your soul and overtook your spirit. I knew that I was losing my stronghold over you as your whispers started getting louder and I heard you repeat Romans 8:28 with clarity and confidence: "And we know that all things work together for good to them that love God, to them who are the called according to his purpose." Danette, I'm a fighter so I know we will probably meet again. Perhaps the next time, I will win. Knowing you, however, even if I did, you would figure out a way to make me become a positive part of your journey. I really don't like that about you but I do respect that you won't allow me to change who you know God has called you to be.

Until next time,
Failed Attempt

Luke 12:6-8 (NIV) Are not five sparrows sold for two pennies? Yet not one of them is forgotten by God. Indeed, the very hairs of your head are all numbered. Don't be afraid; you are worth more than many sparrows. I tell you, whoever acknowledges me before men, the Son of Man will also acknowledge him before the angels of God.

The Sparrow

One of my favorite songs is "His eye is on the sparrow." The chorus reminds us that God not only watches the sparrow but He also watches His children. Often played at home going services, it is a song of hope and encouragement during trying times. One day after hearing the song, my curiosity was peaked. I wondered about the bird that is not only referenced in the song but also in several scriptures in the Bible. What was so special about this particular bird?

According to my research, sparrows are a group of unrelated birds falling into one of three families: Emberizidae, Estrildidae, and Passeridae. The different types of this species, too great to numerate, are found primarily in North and South America; however a few types have also been located in parts of Africa, Europe, and Asia. They range in size and appearance with the smallest documented breed (Chestnut sparrow) measuring 4.5 inches, weighing approximately 13.4g. Feeding on various insects and plants, these adaptable birds prefer to nest in low branches of trees or on the ground. Male sparrows are normally heard singing before they are seen while the females tend to go undetected altogether because the majority of the female species do not sing. Many are considered pests to the agricultural trade and are often used to study adaptability to different climates.

My research revealed that sparrows are pretty insignificant birds. They are not birds that are sought after as pets. They are not on the top of any birdwatcher's list. In biblical days, five together were only worth 2 pennies. Yet, not one of them is forgotten by God. They are special in His eyes. Like the sparrow, there may be times when we feel insignificant but His Word reminds us in Luke 12:7 that He has not forgotten us. We are special in His eyes. Therefore, we are not to be afraid or alarmed. He knows the hairs on our head and values us far above the lowly sparrow. "His eye is on the sparrow and I know He watches me."

If your spirit is feeling hopeless, your heart heavy, and you're discouraged by the trials of life, then today I want to remind you that He sees you and knows your situation. He knows the very hairs on your head and like the sparrow, He cares for you. You are His child and He cares for you. So praise Him in your valley and let the enemy know that YOU are victorious in spite of what it looks like. Be encouraged my friend. God is in charge!

Good Mornin'

Early in my corporate career, I applied for a position in management. I interviewed and was later offered the position. Prior to my start date, my manager invited me into her office. She told me that some members of the interview team were reluctant to hire me for the position because I had a problem with articulation. I was shocked but somehow managed to ask for an explanation. She proceeded to tell me that during my interview, I greeted the panel by saying "Good Mornin" instead of Good Morning.

At the time, I had been a member of the department for a few years, consistently outperformed my work expectations, and had been serving as the department representative for several committees. I was in constant contact with leadership, peers, and internal customers and not once had I received a complaint or concern about my speaking abilities. Yet, during a moment of nervousness, I apparently dropped the "g" off of morning and somehow, some questioned my ability to lead. I asked her if she could provide additional examples. She could not. I thanked her for her feedback and left the office.

I knew that had I not left her office, the conversation would have become combative and unproductive. Instead, I left, headed for the nearest restroom, and prayed for guidance. I was led to use the feedback for my benefit. I enrolled in Toastmasters and learned techniques for dealing with nervousness and anxiety. I gained more experience speaking in front of crowds and discovered how to measure both my tone and volume. An added bonus were the listening exercises that were conducted. My membership in the program helped me build my confidence and removed my fear of public speaking.

It has been over fifteen years since that conversation took place. I have since facilitated numerous workshops, moderated youth panels, served as a guest speaker for several community organizations, and became a business owner. I am thankful for my naysayer. What she used in an attempt to limit me, God used to show me that His power is limitless!

The reality is that we all have naysayers. We may not be able to control what they say, but we can control the impact of their words. Once we accept that man cannot stop what God has planned for us, our naysayers lose their power.

Psa 55:22(NIV) Cast your cares on the Lord and he will sustain you; he will never let the righteous fall.

Going it alone!

When I was in the tenth grade, I constantly butted heads with my shop teacher for reasons that I cannot recall. What made the situation more challenging was that he would be my teacher for the remainder of my high school years. Toward the end of the year, I concocted a plan that would allow me to transfer to another instructor while remaining in the same program. The plan was simple. I would not complete my class work which would cause administration to intercede since I was an honor student with no prior academic issues.

My brilliant plan backfired when I received an F on my report card. What I thought would grab the attention of the administrators actually grabbed the attention of my parents instead. Administration was silent but Mom and Dad had plenty to say. I attempted to explain but it did not go over well. My final grade for the year was a B but that was considered secondary to the matter at hand. I lost my phone privileges and could not have company or go outside. It was summertime and my punishment began immediately. Dad decided that my punishment would not end until my grade improved which meant that I would be on punishment from June until November.

I was a new person that September. I made amends with my teacher and worked hard to improve my grade. My first report card was my ticket to freedom! I received an A in his class. Unfortunately, the big jump from an F to an A along with achieving distinguished honors student further infuriated Dad. He figured that an extension would help me stay on track. The punishment wasn't as stringent. I was able to go out and use the phone on the weekends and attend school related events. I spent my entire junior year on punishment because I thought that I could handle my issue on my own.

Adversity is certain. How we handle it is not. We can devise our own plan and hope for the best; or we can take it before the Lord and let God fight our battle. As a child, I opted for the first choice and suffered an unexpected consequence. I ended up spending a year of my life on punishment when if I had simply gone to my father and discussed the situation with him, he would have handled it.

The beautiful thing about life is that each day contains grace, peace, and mercy from God our Father and the Lord Jesus Christ along with a lesson and a choice. If your lesson today is adversity then I encourage you to give it over to your Heavenly Father and let Him work it out. He can handle it much better than you because He already knows the eventual outcome. So hold fast to Him, praise, worship, and glorify Him and soon, you, too, will witness how He takes what the enemy thought was a setback, and uses it for your good. If, however, you decide to go it alone, be prepared for an unexpected consequence of your action which will lead you right back to your starting point where you will end up doing what He required of you in the first place. It's amazing, but true!

Shake, shake, shake!

One December, I received notification that my laser printer would be replaced the following month and that the toner cartridge for the new printer was not compatible with the current printer. Of course, this notification arrived at the precise time that my current printer's low toner indicator began blinking. I was less than excited at the thought of spending $149.99 for new toner that would be of no use to the office within a month. I decided that instead of replacing the cartridge, I would try a tip that had been shared with me. It required shaking the cartridge to extend its life. So for the next month, prior to printing a document, the cartridge was removed, shook vigorously, and replaced. The result was a crisp and clean printed document every time. Yes, it took a little extra work, but the cartridge had more to give. It just needed a little shake to bring out what was still left.

At times, I feel like life can be similar to the vigorous shake of the toner. Between the challenges, unexpected blows, disappointments, and the trials and tribulations, I've often felt that I have given all that I had to give. That is, until the shake happens. The shaking jolts something in my spirit. It is a connector instructing me not to throw in the towel. The shake keeps me humble and prepares me for the next step of my journey. It tugs at my creativity. It causes me to dig deeper. It causes me to refocus on what is important. It also serves to purge things that aren't good for the journey. The shake has helped me shed self-doubt, insecurity, and lack of motivation. Like the toner, the shakes that I've endured required a little extra work but in end result is that something beautiful emerges; some call it destiny, I call it purpose. Be encouraged and embrace the shakes of life. They won't break you. They will help shape you. To God be the glory!

Graduation Day Class Speaker
(Philadelphia College of Osteopathic Medicine – Organizational
Development and Leadership – Class of 2014)

Good afternoon Dr. Feldstyne, Dr. Vight, Board of Trustee members, faculty, esteemed guests, family, friends, and Class of 2014 graduates! My name is Danette Reid and I am a proud member of the Organizational Development and Leadership (ODL) program. On behalf of my fellow graduates, I am honored and humbled to bring you greetings!

I would first like to thank the faculty for your dedication to our learning. Your commitment to ensuring that we each received a quality education is what sets us apart from the others. You each encouraged us over the years to remain curious, dedicated, and responsible for our learning and today is the culmination of your labor so thank you again!

I would be remiss if I did not thank the support systems represented here today. Whether you are the spouse, significant other, child, parent, sibling, or friend of a graduate, I am thanking you on behalf of my co-learners. Thank you for allowing us the space to grow and encouraging us to keep going when perhaps things got a little tough or when other things attempted to pull the focus off of our work. Your support has been an integral part of our success!

For the past three years, PCOM has been my second home. If asked to describe it in two words, I'd have to say, Life Changing. In his Ted Talk, John Hockenberry, a journalist who happens to be paralyzed talked about intention and making the song your own. For Mr. Hockenberry as well as many of us, life is a journey that can be difficult to navigate. The waters can sometimes be rocky and unpredictable. It is true that we can't always determine what will happen, however, we always have a choice in how to respond. Our response, when done with intention, helps move us into our purpose.

Returning to school was my response to a paralyzing time in my life. My business was in need of reorganization and during the same time, my father-in-law passed away unexpectedly. Those two unpredictable events made something click. I had a choice. I could drink from the woe is me cup or I could take it as a gentle nudging that I was not walking in my purpose. I chose the latter. One of ODL's favorite terms is "Meeting you where you are" and while I don't know exactly what brought each of you to your decision to attend PCOM, I find it amazing that we all showed up and now here we are at a new level in our lives. We aren't the same people we were when we first arrived on campus. Our education has added a new beat to our individual songs. Though our songs are unique, when we sing them together, the harmony we create is capable of changing the world.

Living a life of intention and purpose can be difficult so here are a few things that I'd like to leave with you today:

1 – Everything does not have to be done in a hurry. Slow down and enjoy the simple things in life like an ice cream cone with a friend.

2 – When things become chaotic and life seems to get out of focus, shift the lens. It's probably just a reminder that you are veering off the path.

3 – No one else can be you. Your purpose is your own so accept and embrace it.

4 – Celebrate the small victories. Waiting until you achieve it "ALL" is counterproductive and can wear you out both mentally and physically; and finally

5 – Make the story your own! No one else is responsible for writing your story. Use what you have and when you need more, go out and get it!

Thank you again for your support, be well, and once again congratulations, Class of 2014!

Cheers and Jeers

The people cheered for Him…. "Took branches of palm trees, and went forth to meet him, and cried, Hosanna: Blessed is the King of Israel that cometh in the name of the Lord (John 12:13)."

The same people jeered Him… "But they cried out, Away with him, away with him, crucify him. Pilate saith unto them, Shall I crucify your King? The chief priests answered, We have no king but Caesar. (John 19:15)"

BUT Jesus remained focused! He knew that it was a part of the PLAN. He laid down His life for the very people who proclaimed Him in one breath and denied Him with the next! He laid down His life for you! He laid down His life for me! And on the third day, He rose again… "And as they were afraid, and bowed down their faces to the earth, they said unto them, Why seek ye the living among the dead? He is not here, but is risen: remember how he spake unto you when he was yet in Galilee, saying, The Son of man must be delivered into the hands of sinful men, and be crucified, and the third day rise again" (Luke 24:5-7).

I am humbled knowing that God loves me beyond explanation. He thinks I'm so special that He sent His Son to die for me. On the contrary, there have been times when man has cheered for me and called me friend one minute and denied me the next. Those times were painful and I didn't always handle them as I should. But, I am thankful that experience has taught me to follow Jesus' example and stay focused on the assignment whenever the crowd jeers. I must see things through regardless of man's acceptance or rejection. For in the end, the plan He has for me is much greater than the cheers and jeers of the crowd. And because He is no respecter of persons, the plan He has for you is also greater than the cheers and jeers of your crowd so be encouraged! He loves us beyond explanation and that is more than enough!

CHAPTER 4

Family Matters

It is my opinion that being rich has nothing to do with money. God, family, and friends; yes, that's what makes me one of the richest people in all the land.

Prov 22:6 Train a child in the way he should go, and when he is old he will not turn from it. (NIV)

Date Days

With the blessing of my husband, I go out on dates with someone other than him. My date opens the door for me, helps me to my seat, and allows me to place my order first. One date that I recall was our trip to Dave & Busters. While there, he led the table prayer, waited patiently while I finished eating, and held my hand as we took the stairs to the game room. He was a perfect gentleman! That was, until his competitive nature took over and he showed no mercy as he beat me in every game that we played. Once we exhausted our available credits, we cashed in our tickets for a few trinkets that I am sure were lost before the end of the day. We then walked through the mall, enjoyed a snack, scheduled our next date, and headed back home. Tre' was only nine at the time.

Some say that chivalry is dead. I counter that chivalry is not dead; it is lying dormant because it is no longer being taught. Tre was nowhere near dating age when we started dating. He learned early on how we expected him to behave when the time came for him to start dating young ladies.

As parents, George and I are responsible for setting the standards for our children. It is an awesome responsibility; one that neither of us takes lightly. The Bible instructs parents to train up our children. We cannot allow television, social media, or any other medium to serve as the primary teachers for our young people. It is our responsibility to show our children how to be men and women of God. We must teach them early and often. If we want to witness chivalry among our young men, then we must teach them. If we want to witness young women dressing like respectable young ladies, then we must teach them. If we want to witness peaceful resolution to disagreements among our youth, then we must work with them. If we want our youth to strive for excellence, then we must set the standard. Whatever it is that we feel our youth are lacking, we must place ourselves in a position of teacher and help them figure out how to do it. The job of teacher belongs to us. The Bible shows in Proverbs 22:6 that what we place in our children will not be departed from later in life, so we need to be careful to ensure that what they are taught and who serves as their teacher are both in line with the will and Word of God.

Raising children is an awesome, sometimes overwhelming responsibility. However, teaching our children through our obedience to the Word lays the framework for their future. So instead of feeling that this generation is lost, we must teach them the way to go. Begin with the children in your life. Fall on your knees daily, not only to give thanks to God for your children, but to also ask for His guidance in raising the gift(s) that He has provided. Only then will we begin to restore what has been lying dormant in the younger generation.

Luke 11:9-10(NIV) So I say to you: Ask and it will be given to you; seek and you will find; know and the door will be opened to you. For everyone who ask receives; he who seeks finds; and to him who knocks, the door will be opened.

"Super woman" v. "The Needy"

"Anyone desiring prayer, please make your way to the altar." This is a sentence I've heard practically every time I attended church since the age of ten. I used to watch people make their way to the front, and as a brazen teen, I remember thinking how needy the regulars (the ones who went up every week) must have been since they seemed to have needed prayer for everything. When I reached my twenties, I added invincibility to my list of descriptors and thought that I had strength that matched the famous superhero, Superwoman. I was self-reliant and I really believed that I walked around with an "S" on my chest! I rarely went to God publicly for anything. I talked to Him a few times a week but my talks were brief. I would be sure to include a generic thank you, a short praise, and if there was something I needed, a request. I never strayed from the script; it was always in that order. There was no need for me to be wasting His time carrying things to Him that I knew I could handle on my own. I used to wonder what could be so challenging that those needy people who have to approach the altar each and every week because in my mind they weren't using the tools that they had been given to problem solve. In my youth, I guess one could say that I had placed God in a box that should only be opened in case of emergency.

My emergency arrived at the age of thirty. I was thirty-three weeks pregnant with our son when I felt a slight cramp in my side but I was Superwoman so I was not alarmed. It wasn't until two hours later when I had doctors surrounding me trying to stop my labor that I considered that Superwoman was indeed an alter ego that may not stand up to the current test at hand. I tried to maintain my false sense of being in control until the lead doctor announced that I would be delivering our baby that day. I remember asking about the risks of my premature delivery and being told that they could not make any promises. George Reid, III was born about fifteen minutes after that brief conversation and whisked out of the room by a team of neonatal nurses and doctors before I even had a chance to hold him.

Later that evening after everyone had gone home, I felt frightened and alone. For the first time in my adult life, I felt completely vulnerable. The "S" that I wore on my chest had vanished. I cried out the words that I had heard uttered repeatedly by the needy over the years: "Jesus, help me. I can't do this by myself. I need you." I stayed in bed that night with tears streaming down my face wondering if God heard the prayer of His daughter. For the first time in my life, September 6, 1999 to be exact, I went to God authentically and humbled.

The next day, George needed surgery. He had air in his chest pocket. Again I cried, prayed, and humbled myself in His presence. This became my routine for the next seventeen days while our little guy remained in the neonatal intensive care unit. The daily tears were cleansing and washed away my superwoman mentality. I was vulnerable. I visited the hospital chapel every day and solicited prayers for my family. I had become the needy person that I laughed at in my youth. I began going to God for everything big and small. On September 23, 1999, George left the hospital with a clean bill of health.

George's early arrival was a pivotal moment in my adult life. It helped me realize that the needy folk are actually the smart ones. They know how to take their concerns to God and trust Him to take care of them. They are not afraid to show their vulnerability for they recognize that being vulnerable to God allows Him room to shape and direct lives. The needy recognize that God, not the individual is the supplier. I had it backwards as a child. The superwoman with the invincible attitude does not stand a chance against the needy because the needy have the almighty power of our God working on their behalf while the superwoman is limited in her powers. I am grateful to God for keeping me during my superwoman phase. I am even more grateful to now humbly count myself as one of his needy children.

If you find yourself thinking that you can walk this path alone, I urge you to realize that your true strength lies in trusting God to direct your life. Your limited power is no match for what He can do in your life.

George

Our children have kept us busy throughout their childhood. Danae' was a cheerleader, played in the band, ushered at church, was active in extracurricular activities and like her mother, was a social butterfly and always at one event or another. George was equally involved. He played sports year-round (football, basketball, & baseball) since the age of five, played in the orchestra, belonged to the Y and was also an usher at church. Unlike Danae', George is our homebody so our home serves at the hangout spot for his crew.

Today's media often highlights the absent father, the jailed father, the aloof father; but rarely do we get a glimpse of the active and engaged father. In honor of my husband who has never missed an activity, rarely missed a parent teacher conference, attends every practice, taught our children how to drive, etc. and all fathers who are hardworking, active, dependable and present in their children's lives, I have decided to utilize some space to publically say thanks! You are indeed one of the world's most precious jewels.

Thank you for providing for your children. Thank you for showing love through your actions. Thank you for putting your family first. Thank you for doing what others may view as nontraditional like being a stay at home dad or leaving work early to care for a sick child. Thank you for playing dolls with your daughters and attending their tea parties. Thank you for being the last one to shut your eyes at night to ensure that your family is safe. Thank you for sitting in the ER all night even though you can't stand the sight of blood when your son hurt himself on a dare. Thank you for sharing words of wisdom with your daughters when they need to know the games that boys play. Thank you for teaching your sons how to become men. Thank you for being you. We don't say it often enough, but to all the dads who are reading this, YOU ROCK! Thank you and thank you again for being the fabric that keeps your family together.

I Peter 4: 10 – 11 (NLT) ¹⁰ God has given each of you a gift from his great variety of spiritual gifts. Use them well to serve one another. ¹¹ Do you have the gift of speaking? Then speak as though God himself were speaking through you. Do you have the gift of helping others? Do it with all the strength and energy that God supplies. Then everything you do will bring glory to God through Jesus Christ. All glory and power to him forever and ever! Amen.

What's in your box?

When my son was six years old, we celebrated with a party at a local kid friendly venue. George or Tre' as he preferred to be called at the time had a great time celebrating with his friends. When it was gift time, he excitedly ripped open his gifts. He was happy to show off the contents of each gift, holding them high in the air for all to see. This pattern continued until he opened a box that contained a nice outfit but no toy. Unlike the others, this gift wasn't held up in the air. He tossed the gift to the side and moved on to the next one while I sat there completely mortified at his unbecoming behavior. I didn't want to ruin his special day so we didn't discuss what happened until after the party was over. I explained to him that it was rude to disregard what he had been given and that I never expected to witness or hear about him displaying that type of behavior again. He apologized and we moved past the situation.

God, like Tre's gift giver, took special care to provide each of us with spiritual gifts that are unique and of great variety. He blessed me with the gift of writing and inspiring while for others, he gave gifts of singing, performing, organizing, leading, etc. God decided how to disperse the gifts and intends for us to use them to bless others and give Him glory. Unfortunately, many of us treat our gifts like Tre' treated his clothes because the gift He gave us isn't the one that we wanted. So instead of blessing others with the gifts that He placed in us, we attempt to step into areas that weren't designated for us. Then we become frustrated when they don't have the impact that we thought they would. Meanwhile, the gifts that He has given sit idle and unused.

God is all-knowing and gave each of us the gifts that He wanted us to have. Most gifts will not place you in the forefront; however, your gifts are not in place so that you are recognized, they are to be used for building His Kingdom and for His glory. They are uniquely yours and whether they are gifts of organization, inspiring others, visiting the sick, or cleaning up the sanctuary, they are important and need to be shared. You were specifically chosen to receive and use them by none other than God Himself. What He has placed in you is there to touch someone else. If you withhold your gift, then you are withholding God's goodness from those who need it.

Today, I encourage you to open your box and see what gift you've tossed to the side. Look at your gift through God's eyes and ask that He breathe life into it so that you can carry out I Peter 4: 10 – 11 in a manner that is pleasing to our Heavenly Father. The impact your gift has is much greater than you can imagine!

John 8:7 (KJV) So when they continued asking him, he lifted up himself, and said unto them, He that is without sin among you, let him first cast a stone at her.

Happy Anniversary Charlene!

September 12th is my sister, Charlene and her husband's wedding anniversary.

In 2009, I recall reaching out to her about a week after her anniversary just to say hello. She was unavailable but promised to call me later. The call never came. I followed up with a text message, but again she did not respond. Finally, on September 20, 2009, I made my third attempt and successfully connected with my baby sister. We had an enjoyable conversation, probably our third or fourth since her anniversary. As the call drew to a close, I joked that because she neglected to call me back nor respond to my text message that she may find herself the subject of a future writing about appropriate response time. I chuckled until she responded with "You need to write about yourself. I've talked to you a few times in the past week and you never mentioned my anniversary." Yikes! I knew that her anniversary was on the twelfth. In fact, my sister Chariesse and I discussed her anniversary when we spoke earlier that week. Somehow, the sun not only rose and set, but did so for eight days and honestly, would have continued to do so without an utterance of recognition from me regarding her special day. I had no excuse. I forgot about her special day. I apologized and wished her a Happy Belated Anniversary before ending the call.

Later that evening as I strolled the neighborhood for my daily exercise, my mind wandered to the story of the woman who was brought before Jesus by the Scribes and Pharisees for committing the sin of adultery. They requested Jesus' thoughts regarding an acceptable punishment and reminded Him that under the Law of Moses, this sin was punishable by stoning. Jesus continued to write on the ground, ignoring the original request for a punishment, but they persisted. When He chose to respond, He simply stated that the first stone should be thrown by the one who has not sinned (John 8:7). Soon, each person assembled there felt convicted and retreated leaving only Jesus and the accused woman. Jesus did not condemn her, He told her to "go and sin no more (John 8:11)"

That day I acted like the Scribes and Pharisees. I told her of her offense without considering the ones that I had committed. When she reminded me of my offense, I realized how easy it is to judge someone else while thinking you are without sin. Thankfully, my error was not a life changing blunder but the magnitude has stayed with me over the years: "He that is without sin among you, let him cast the first stone at her (John 8:7)." No one is perfect and that includes both you and me. We have all fallen short, and it is only the redeeming power of Jesus Christ that keeps us.

John 3:20 – 21 For every wrongdoer hates (loathes, detests) the Light, and will not come out into the Light but shrinks from it, lest his works (his deeds, his activities, his conduct) be exposed and reproved. 21But he who practices truth [who does what is right] comes out into the Light; so that his works may be plainly shown to be what they are--wrought with God [divinely prompted, done with God's help, in dependence upon Him].

Cupid, you can't hide!

Cupid, our big lovable dog, was a lab mix and weighed at least seventy pounds. He thought he was a lap dog and loved nothing more than to be around the family. He would follow the kids everywhere except the kitchen and family room, two places he was not allowed. His favorite place during the day was wherever the kids were and at night, he slept in the hallway between their rooms. Whenever he was home alone, we could be sure that Cupid would eagerly meet us at the door upon our return unless he sensed that he was in trouble. Cupid loved attention as long as it was positive attention. As a young dog, Cupid would sometimes let his curiosity get the best of him. Some of the great no-no's that he enjoyed were chewing socks, jumping on the futon in the guest room, and turning over the garbage can. He knew that he would be reprimanded so if he did any of the above, he would attempt to hide. Any time that he wasn't waiting for us at the door, we knew to start looking around the house to see what damage he caused. He never seemed to grasp that his actions always told that he behavior was less than stellar and that he couldn't hide from us. When we located the damage, he would be reprimanded but soon after, he would return to the happy go lucky dog that we adored.

God knows His children far more intimately than we ever knew Cupid. He knows our comings and goings; our ups and downs; and has taken account of every hair on each of our heads. He knows that we are going to show Him our best selves. We come into the light to show ourselves when things are right in our lives. Like Cupid, we attempt to hide from God when we have done wrong. We may be able to fool one another, but we can't fool Him. He's known us since before we were placed into our mother's womb. He knows when we've fallen short. He knows when things are out of place in our lives. Thankfully, He is a forgiving God and though we may have a consequence for our wrongdoings, He will continue to love and guide us through our correction and repentance.

My challenge to you is that you take to God all those things that you believe you are hiding from Him and offer Him yourself as a gift. Ask for forgiveness and for His help to cleanse those areas of your life that cause you to hide from His loving embrace. We have all fallen short in some area and until we fully expose ourselves to Jesus and ask that He work it out, we will continue to walk in the dark even if we've fooled ourselves into thinking otherwise.

(This piece was written in 2010. It has been included here in memory of our awesome and faithful four legged friend, Cupid.)

Prov 18:13 (NIV) He who answers before listening- that is his folly and his shame.

Quick Response

It was a cold day in the winter of 2012 when I tweeted the following: "Midweek Motivation, Trouble in Cupid Land is now available @ www. jewelsfrommyjourney.com." Within minutes, I received a response advising me to love myself first. The post then referred me to several websites geared toward self-esteem building and valuing one self. Initially, I did not correlate my original tweet with the response I had received. It later dawned on me that the title may have led someone to believe that I had reached out to Twitter® for relationship advice. It was evident that this person did not access the website because if they did, they would have known that Cupid was my fun-loving dog and that the prior week's motivation was not about relationships. While I was appreciative of the assistance offered, albeit for a problem that I was not having, it left me to wonder how often we jump to conclusions when we base our opinion on limited information.

In this day of technology where social media is king, breaking news is all the rage, and texting reigns supreme, we, as Christians, must be careful that we don't fall into the trap of making haste decisions or offering quick responses when we are not equipped with the full story. The Bible tells us that we must first listen to the entire story before responding or end up filled with folly and shame (Prov 18:13). I am guilty of jumping to conclusions more than I care to admit. So, to avoid this pitfall in the future, I have committed to evaluating the information given; gathering additional information when available; and asking pointed questions to gain a full understanding of what I believe to be the facts. Only then will I offer a response. Yes, it may take me a little longer to respond, however, I'd rather take my time responding than respond quickly and possibly lead someone down the wrong path and be left filled with folly and shame. I invite you to do the same.

Pro 18:24(KJV) A man that hath friends must shew himself friendly: and there is a friend that sticketh closer than a brother.

Close Friendship

Within the first few weeks of her seventh grade year, my soft spoken daughter morphed into an outspoken, confident, stylish & popular young lady. She made new friends, developed new interests, and found herself with a full social calendar. But her newfound popularity was not without drama. On several occasions, she had strong disagreements with her best friend since first grade. For the first time in six years, they each struggled with where they fit in each other's lives. They had become accustomed to spending all of their free time together and the new mix of friends they each made, combined with different interests, and varied social calendars was a major challenge for their friendship. They weren't spending as much time together and each began to feel insecure believing that their friendship was fading. After many discussions with Danae', I found the core of the problem was that they each believed that their friendship entitled them to dictate to one another who they could be friends with, how they should act, and where they should go. This belief led to many arguments, hurt feelings, and almost ruined a strong friendship.

As her mother, my role was to listen with an unbiased ear and provide feedback that would help her grow and become a better friend. I often shared with her what I learned over the years, sometimes the hard way, about friendship. I would tell her that true friends are a gift from God. They will be by your side through life's challenges; support you as you grow; and love you even when they don't agree with you. I would often pause at this moment so that she could absorb the lesson before continuing. I'd then explain that true friends won't try to run your life; they will instead offer you advice but leave it to you to make the decision. She'd normally interrupt me at this point and state that she didn't want her friendship to end. I would smile and say something like "I know baby, now listen to what I didn't realize until I was married with children. True friends are comfortable with their place in your life and will not force you to spend every waking moment with them in order to prove your friendship. They are an extension of your family and having them in your life is a blessing. They may not always be in your life so you have to bless God for whatever time you have with them."

Friendships are indeed a blessing from God. They are a treasure and while we all want the best for our friends, we must be careful not to try to control one another. It is not our job to determine how a friend must spend their time, who they can be friends with, or where they should go. Our job is to love, pray for, and be a support system to one another along this journey. We have to let our friendships grow naturally over time and remember that God and God alone is the head of their life and Director of their path.

If you are currently struggling with your friendships, then I encourage you to define what it means to be a friend. Jesus is the ultimate example so start there. Look at His life and how He treated His friends. Watch how He allowed them to grow; how He practiced forgiveness, and how He continued to love them through their shortcomings. He had the power to make them servant, but He chose to call them friend. Use the example of His life as a barometer for how you treat your friends. To have a friend, you must first be one.

CHAPTER 5

Only believe....

My travel plan is simple. I go wherever He leads me! I am freed from my past, loving the present, and looking forward to the future because God is leading the way.

Are You Sure?

"God has spoken, let the church say Amen." This song, by the late Andre Crouch featuring Pastor Marvin Winans is one of my favorite gospel songs. It speaks to my heart every time I hear it on the radio. It reminds me of times past when instead of "amen," my reply used to be "are you sure?" I used to believe that I was in charge of my life. I often assumed that God got his wires crossed whenever it rained in my life. In hindsight, I recognize how foolish it was for me to believe that He would make countless mistakes when it came to my life. Perhaps more foolish were my attempts to orchestrate a different outcome than what He intended. Thankfully, experience and growth have taught me that I am not exempt from heartache, disappointment, and challenges. The Bible tells me that it rains on the just and unjust (Matt 5:45). Expecting to escape the rain because I am one of His children is unrealistic and trying to manipulate a situation to achieve my desired outcome is unacceptable. He uses every situation for my good and whenever I get in the way, I delay what He has for me. I have since learned to say "Amen" and allow God to be God over my life.

If you are in a place where you think God has made a mistake, please know that He has not forgotten about you. What He has promised you will come to pass. What He has spoken may not always feel good but it is preparing you for the next step on your journey. It may be raining in your life right now but God is still present and has already arranged for your ultimate victory. So, my friend, put a smile on your face, carry a song in your heart, be encouraged and offer God a hearty "Amen."

My Coach

The coaches are on the field; my son, the quarterback, is on the ground. That last play was a doozy! A player from the opposing team knocked the wind out of George as he was attempting a pass. He was down before the whistle blew and a hush fell across the crowd. I don't know when I stopped breathing but I know that I didn't start again until he was up and walking off the field. Once he reached the sideline, his coaches took care of him. Eventually, he went back into the game and led his team to a win, proving that being down doesn't equal being out.

Life is a lot like football. We all want to avoid the knock downs so we develop goals and implement our plays. But as is the case with George and his team, even the best laid plans in our lives don't always get executed exactly as we would like. Stuff happens. Jobs are lost. Relationships are challenged. Resources run low. Sickness invades the body. A loved one dies unexpectedly. The list of stuff that might impact one's plan is endless. When stuff happens, it literally feels like the wind has been knocked out of your sails and you have to make a choice. You can lay on the field or you can call for help?

When life happened for me, I used to lay on the field and wait for the game to be called. I would wave my flag and quit. Watching my son get back up with the help of his coaches caused a shift in my life. It changed my perspective and showed me that I was forgetting to call my coach. Jesus is my coach and He promised never to leave or forsake me. In times of trouble, I now call on Him. As He ushers me off the field to get me ready for the next play, He reminds me of His promises and refills my hope tank. He helps me see that the knock downs of life are par for the course but they won't knock me out; they just knock me to my knees and draw me even closer to Him.

God's grace and mercy is sufficient and much larger than any problem you face. If you are currently battling the stuff of life, be encouraged and know that your Coach is waiting to help you off the field. Don't stay in a place of defeat, give it to Him and let Him fill you with hope and remind you of His promises.

Luke 7:21-23 (NIV) At that very time Jesus cured many who had diseases, sicknesses and evil spirits, and gave sight to many who were blind. ²²So he replied to the messengers, "Go back and report to John what you have seen and heard: The blind receive sight, the lame walk, those who have leprosy[a] are cured, the deaf hear, the dead are raised, and the good news is preached to the poor. ²³Blessed is the man who does not fall away on account of me."

Jury Duty

On November 2, 2009 at 8:15am, I checked in at the County Courthouse to fulfill my civic duty. There were fifty-one of us assembled in the juror room and chances were that at least twelve of us would be called to decide the fate of someone else. The day started with a video, followed by a welcome from one of the judges before being told to sit and wait for further instruction. Soon, one hour gave way to three with no further instruction from the court. We recessed for lunch and then sat a while longer. Finally, at 2:15 pm, we were excused due to a last minute guilty plea. If I didn't know better, I would have believed that I spent a whole day confined for nothing but I knew that wasn't the case.

After lunch, my intention was to sit in the back of the room and read a book. However, God had something different planned. Before I could pull the book out of my bag, I found myself in a deep conversation with two women who were walking a similar path and they were pessimistic about the outcome. One woman suppressed her dreams because someone told her it wasn't possible and she accepted their report, while the other thought it best not to dream at all because the chances of them coming true were slim to none.

I laughed to myself thinking "God, all I want to do is read this book and mind my business." I knew that wasn't an option so I shared with them what I know to be true: Man does not have the final say on what happens in our lives, God does. I encouraged them to surround themselves with positive people and affirm themselves every day. I was then asked how I maintain a positive outlook and I replied that it's because I know how the story ends. When it ends, I win because it all works together for my good and with Him all things are possible so I can walk boldly in my purpose and not allow the naysayers to permeate my spirit, even when I am my own naysayer which was the case with the second woman. Shortly thereafter, the jury supervisor dismissed us. The three of us left the courthouse together begin our journey back to our own lives, each of us having been touched by the other. We wished each other well and parted ways.

Later in the evening I wondered what my life would be like if I let the dream killers have their way. Would I be happily married? Would my children be who they are? Would I be running a business? Would I be writing? Would I be working to empower our young women? What would have happened if I accepted the report of those who told me that my dreams were unrealistic and therefore unachievable? Where would I be? What would I be doing? I'd probably be living a life that wasn't fulfilling or purposeful. Today, I am grateful for parents who always encouraged me to dream big. They taught me to believe that my dreams are achievable because nothing is too hard for God. So when the dream killers came along as I was growing and maturing, I knew not to accept their report because they did not have the final say in my life.

If you find yourself struggling with fulfilling your dreams because someone told you that you were being unrealistic, then I encourage you to accept the report of the Lord. He will work all things for your good but you must trust Him to direct your path. If He has revealed it to you, He will bring it to pass. Nothing is too big for Him for it is He who gave sight to the blind; made the lame walk, and raised folk from the dead (Luke 7:22). Be encouraged and continue to dream big.

Prov 3:5-6 (KJV) Trust in the LORD with all thine heart; and lean not unto thine own understanding. In all thy ways acknowledge him, and he shall direct thy paths.

Today, I understood!

Tears adorned a beautiful woman's face as I shared what she wrote with the group. I wanted to say something but could not find my voice. I witnessed the pain that held her captive. The only thing I could think to do was to give her a hug and let her know that she is not alone. She dabbed at her tears and managed a smile. Hope for a brighter day is what she is found today. Her smile grows even brighter and I am humbled by the power of God in the room.

When I began writing, I had no idea that my words would create a safe space for others. Honestly, it was a path that I wasn't sure that I wanted to take. At the time, I didn't feel qualified to share anything because I was a mess. I spent most of 2007 walking through the valley and was afraid to share my vulnerability with others. After much prayer and wrestling with Proverbs 3:5-6, I sent out my first Midweek Motivation email in 2007.

Two years after that first email, my purpose came into focus. My obedience to begin sharing my writing led me to the creation of Midweek Motivation. Midweek Motivation led me to self-publish *Jewels From My Journey. Jewels From My Journey* led me to the creation of "Jewels" & Tea book signings. The "Jewels" & Tea book signings led me to the creation of the About Me game. The About Me writing game led to the shedding of a piece of baggage that another woman was carrying. It was baggage that weighed her down and God knew that she would need the company and comfort of a group of supportive women in order to release it. My valley was connected to her breakthrough. How awesome is our God that He would know all of this before either of us were placed in our mother's wombs? It is a humbling thought.

God's plan is often very different from our own and though we may struggle with accepting what He allows, I want to encourage you to be obedient. Use Proverbs 3:5-6 as your guide. Let it speak to your heart! Understand that God can use anyone and at some point, it will be your turn. You may not understand it but trust God. He will neither leave nor forsake you and will use your experience to bless someone else!

Lane Living

I once made two salads of unequal portions for lunch. The larger salad was for my husband and the smaller one was for me. I intentionally stored them in different sized containers and advised my husband which container belonged to him. He nodded in agreement; however, when the time came for him to go to work, he took the wrong salad. He eats a larger portion than I do so unfortunately because he took something that wasn't prepared for him, he wasn't satisfied with his lunch. I, on the other hand had more salad than I could possibly consume. I'm sure it was accidental. He didn't intend to covet what was intended for me....

Ex 20:17 "Thou shalt not covet thy neighbour's house, thou shalt not covet thy neighbour's wife, nor his manservant, nor his maidservant, nor his ox, nor his ass, nor any thing that is thy neighbour's." (KJV)

Looking at how another person's life appears to be often brings about a covetous spirit. The desire to be in "perfect" relationships, amass a certain level of perceived wealth, etc. can lead one down an unintended path. If left to fester, the desire turns to coveting and poor decision making in an effort to acquire the object no matter the cost. However once received, one quickly finds that they are not equipped to handle what has been acquired. Whether it is a car or house payment that one can't afford; a relationship that is on unequal footing or a job that brings misery, the object coveted is insufficient for its intended purpose, leading to many sorrows. This occurs because it was not intended for the person who received it. It belonged to someone else. There's a gospel song whose words ring clear and true "What God has for me, it is for me." Another person can try to take it, but the result won't be the same. In other words, we need to be mindful to remember that what God has for us is more than enough. We should not fool ourselves into believing that God made a mistake when He was handing out the blessings. In the end, my hubby, bless his heart, experienced a hard lesson that ultimately left him dissatisfied. That day he learned the benefit of lane living. Stay in your lane. You cannot own what does not belong to you. You can covet it but in the end, you will regret your choice. Trust God. He knows exactly what He is doing.

CHAPTER 6

Forgiveness

Sin is forgivable, not justifiable. Be sure not to confuse the two.

Unmarked Grave

His grave was unmarked but with the help of my son, I read the map and within moments, I stood at the site of the man whose blood runs through my veins. Standing there at his grave, I wondered about the life he lived. Was he happy? Did he have regret? Did he ever wonder about his children? I stood there knowing that my questions would never be answered by him. I stood there knowing that this was no longer about a class assignment for my Masters' program, this was about unlocking a piece of me and learning how to forgive. The bitterness I felt for him was neatly tucked in a space reserved for my deepest hurt. Though he died before I was born, I wanted to have wonderful stories and traditions passed down to me by the patriarch of the family. Sadly, that was not the case. I stood at the grave that day and forgave him for leaving my father when he was three. I thanked him for giving me the awesome gift of my father. I felt bad for him because he didn't get to see the man that my father had become. I then laid a flower arrangement on the unmarked grave and thought of the irony that he was buried just a few miles away from the place I lived during my days as an undergraduate student at West Chester University of Pennsylvania. I took one last look at the ground that held the man I never knew and walked away in peace.

James Eastland. I bore his surname but he was a stranger to me. Through my assignment, I learned that he was a painter born in 1902 in a little town in South Carolina. He passed away at the age of 65 in Philadelphia, PA a year before my birth. No longer a stranger, I found love for him that day. He is my family. He is my grandfather. Rest well, Grandfather Eastland.

Forgiveness is freeing.

Doing Time

There is a prison that keeps you bound.

Bitterness is your warden.

Guarding everyone with extreme caution is your cell.

Seeing the glass as half empty is the meal you eat three times a day.

The chip on your shoulder is your cellmate.

A hardened heart is what keeps you from being paroled.

The prison that you are living in is un-forgiveness. You are holding on to what someone did to bring you harm. You have decided that no one else will ever get that close to you. You feel justified by your actions.

You haven't considered the fact that your un-forgiveness continues to give the offender power over you. You haven't considered that your un-forgiveness prevents you from fully experiencing what God has designed for your life. You haven't considered that your other relationships suffer because you find it hard to trust anyone.

Only you can free yourself from this prison. Forgiveness is freeing. It takes back your power. It helps you find your smile. It is the beginning of peace. Open your heart and set yourself free. Forgiveness is not about the person who offended you; forgiveness is about you!

Matt 6:14-15(NIV): For if you forgive men when they sin against you, your heavenly Father will also forgive you. But if you do not forgive men their sins, your Father will not forgive your sins.

Junk Drawer

The onset of springtime brings an intense need for me to deep clean my house. I do a little each day with the plan of having a spotless home by the first week of spring. It is a ritual that I started years ago with the birth of my firstborn, Danae'. One morning, I remember getting up early to work on the kitchen. I cleaned the fridge, scrubbed the appliances and swept the floor before taking a break to open the blinds and decide which music to play next. Before becoming too relaxed, I started on my next task which was to clean out the junk drawer. It had been at least six months since I'd last attacked the drawer. I reasoned that it would be a simple job since I had already cleaned it during the latter part of the prior year. I recall sorting through the drawer deciding what needed to stay and what needed to be trashed or recycled. I came across several receipts and coupons while cleaning and wondered why I still had them since they had expired over a year ago. It then hits me! I am not a cleaner, I am a concealer. I do the same thing with my pocket books. When I change bags, I move junk from one bag to the next, never really cleaning it out. When I unpack my luggage after a trip, I never remove the labels. I wait until the next trip and the baggage attendant removes them for me. I could go on with my list as I am thinking of all the things that I either move or conceal but never actually remove. At that moment, I promised myself that I would work on this bad habit. Thankfully, this concealing spirit no longer lives in other areas of my life.

Prior to casting all of my cares at the feet of my Lord and Savior, Jesus Christ, I used to battle with a concealing spirit, especially in the area of forgiveness. I would tell myself that I forgave someone who wronged me. I would convince myself that I had moved beyond a situation. However, at the first sign of a new issue, whoever was the object of my current situation was made to pay for all that was in my past. I don't recall the actual day or experience that forced me to no longer use a laundry list approach to dealing with issues. But something happened because I now seek to deal with each situation as an unrelated series of events; and my life has been richer because of it.

I am not perfect but I have learned that there is power in forgiveness. When I forgive, I am freed to live life not weighed down with the troubles of this world. My life is filled with Jesus joy because I understand that He has forgiven me for my sins and in turn, expects me not only to forgive those who have committed offenses against me but to also obey His commandment to love others. I do not always get it right, but I am intentional about dedicating myself to His principles. Now if only I can do the same with the material things! I guess I will have to keep that in prayer.

Summer 2013

I ran into a bully from my youth back in the summer of 2013. I didn't show any emotion until I was no longer in that person's presence. As soon as I reached my car, tears of frustration poured down my face. As the events of my past were pulled into the forefront of my thoughts, a rage that I had never experienced appeared front and center. I thought about revenge. I thought about exacting a plan that would make my former bully pay for all the ways that I was made to feel inferior in my youth. I thought about how those actions contributed to my adult life. I thought about how I vowed never to allow a bully to appear in my children's life. I thought about the satisfaction I would experience by creating a demise for this person. I thought about the power my bully still had over me without my knowledge. I was paralyzed in those moments. I prayed and prayed and prayed some more. The days following that encounter are still a blur. I remember going to church one Sunday a few weeks later with my open wound. I remember thinking of the fake apology that was offered that day; an apology that I accepted so that I could end the awkwardness I was feeling. I prayed to God to help me let this go. The response given wasn't the one I was expecting. It was a whisper of forgiveness. In order to move forward, I had to forgive my bully and walk away with my head held high. God showed me that my anger and the way that I had been acting since running into that individual was placing a wedge in my walk with God.

I struggled with the decision to forgive. I read and re-read scripture passages about forgiveness. I held onto my feelings for a while longer. I asked God to be patient with me. I told Him that I needed Him to help me. He kept sending me back to the same scriptures. He encouraged me to shed the baggage. He helped me take the power away from my bully by having me share my story with my trusted circle. He hugged me through the smile of friends. He reminded me that His Son forgave those who had sinned against him and that I needed to do the same. It took me a while, honestly, longer than I care to admit, but eventually, I forgave my bully. In doing so, the pain of my past lost its edge and I was freed to live a more fulfilling present. Today, I bless God for staying with me while I worked through that valley experience.

I share this with you to acknowledge that sometimes forgiveness is a process. It's not always easy and is often, downright challenging. But if you don't forgive, it gives another person the power to control you even if you are not fully aware that this is happening. Forgiveness is not about the person who offended you; forgiveness is about you! If you are struggling with forgiving someone, ask God to help you! He will set the plan in motion. Be encouraged.

Forgiveness is freeing.

CHAPTER 7

Let's Grow Together – A month of life changing thoughts

In 2015, thirty-eight days before the New Year, I set out on an intentional journey to end the year with true thanksgiving in my heart. That period allowed me to look at things through a different lens. During that time, I experienced both highs and lows. Every day was not filled with sunshine and in fact, I experienced some stressful moments and had to make a few tough decisions. Surprisingly, I was so focused on being grateful that those experiences did not have the power to cause me to become ungrateful. I learned that when you change your focus, you change your life. Even though everyday was and is not filled with sunshine, it was and will always be filled with the Son who shines. The following pages contain thirty days of little gems that have helped me begin the year afresh and anew. I pray that they meet you where you are and help you along your journey.

Day One: A small mind cannot comprehend a big dream. Don't allow the negative noise of others to stop you from dreaming and pursuing what God has for you.

Day Two: If you don't respect your own boundaries, no one else will either.

Day Three: Having more requires more from you. Be sure that you are willing and able to nurture, maintain, and be accountable for that which you ask for.

Day Four: There is no mandatory requirement stating that you must participate in drama.

Day Five: Your situation is not new. It is just new to you! Find a mentor and be one too.

Day Six: Today is Day Six. You are either six days closer to your goal or six days farther away. Procrastination will rob you of your accomplishment if you give it time.

Day Seven: Situations you found yourself in Years Ago will continue to find their way in your Years To Go if you don't learn the lesson that it was meant to teach and adjust your response accordingly.

Day Eight: Planned excuses take too much time and energy. A simple No will do.

Day Nine: Never give power to the noise of your haters. They're doing their job. Somebody has to build that footstool for your feet (Matt 22:44). Keep pushing!

Day Ten: The things of this day are already predestined for God knew about this day when I was yet in the womb. Therefore, I shall go with the flow because I know that I am His and He is guiding me.

Day Eleven: Would you enjoy sleeping in your bed if it were made of the words you speak? Would it be cold and uninviting or would it be warm and welcoming? Would it be as hard as bricks or as soft as feathers or somewhere in-between depending on to whom you were speaking? The bed you make will be the bed in which you lay so consider what you say before you speak.

Day Twelve: A person can have a different opinion but that doesn't mean they're bad. A person can make a different choice but that doesn't make them unworthy of being loved. A person can make a mistake but that doesn't mean they're hell bound. A person can be different from you and you can decide not to judge them. At some point in your life, you will be that person for someone else. Extend the same grace and mercy that you wish to receive.

Day Thirteen: Take off the mask and be real with yourself even if you choose not to be real with anyone else. Make the tough decisions that take you out of your comfort zone. Dare to listen to the whisper and nudging of the Spirit within. Be clear about your intention. Take time for you. Say please and thanks. Take risks. Challenge yourself to be better. Be kind to yourself. It's your journey so own it.

Day Fourteen: Help without looking for credit. Assist without expectation that it will be reciprocated. Do your part even if no one else does their part. Live healthy. Be happy. Laugh a lot. Remember that everything does not have to be politicized. People are different. You choose who you allow in your circle. Protect your mind, body, and soul by choosing wisely. Allow God to handle the rest.

Day Fifteen: The person with the best hand doesn't always win. The person with the bad hand doesn't always lose. How one plays their hand is what matters. Always play like you will win no matter which hand you currently hold. Be encouraged!

Day Sixteen: Some people are very unhappy about the storm. Some people aren't happy about the storm but have made plans to adapt and adjust. Some people are happy about the storm and looking forward to making snow angels, drinking hot chocolate, spending time with family, and making memories. Perspective is everything. Same storm, different outcomes.

Day Seventeen: Last night after work my old friend, Relaxation, knocked on my door and said hey girl! We got snowed in together so she said she had to stay for the weekend. We've been side by side from the moment she arrived. I think I'm going to invite her to move in. Guess it's time to check the calendar and see what needs to come off so that I have more time to spend with my old friend.

Day Eighteen: Do the hardest thing on your to-do list first. You get it out of the way and it is smooth sailing from there.

Day Nineteen: Sometimes your adversary may be dressed as a "friend." Love them anyway. Sometimes your adversary is direct and lets you know that they're not a fan favorite. Pray for them anyway. When you are walking in purpose, you are bound to have adversaries. Smile, blow air kisses, and keep on walking. Your battle is already won and the very ones trying to keep you down will be the ones that will be made your footstool.

Day Twenty: I wear many hats so a To-Do list is essential for me. I used to just look at it as a checklist of things to accomplish. However in recent years, I came to understand the beauty of the list. Its true purpose is to show me when I am getting away from my purpose and priorities. When it becomes filled with "stuff," I know that I have lost my focus and need to make adjustments. It reminds me that No is a complete sentence. It reminds me that I am but one person and every project does not require my participation. It tells me that if I am overbooked, then I am spending less time nurturing my relationships with my husband, children, family and close friends. It tells me that I haven't made time for what's important. It tells me to stop and smell the roses! I love my To-Do list and today is one of those days that I needed all of the reminders. So, my friends, what is your list telling you??

Day Twenty-One: Plan. Create Action Steps. Execute. Adjust if necessary. Re-execute. Adjust if necessary. Execute again. Adjust if necessary. Execute again. Are you getting the gist? Don't give up! If God gave it to you, it shall come to pass. Giving up in the middle is not an option. Be encouraged and keep pushing.

Day Twenty-Two: In order to grow, a seed must first be planted. The seed of a new friendship is a simple hello. The seed of change is open and honest communication. The seed of great leadership is to always ask yourself if you would follow you. The seed of the family is agape love. Likewise, the seed of disconnection is lost communication. The seed of confusion is dishonesty. The seed of complacency is becoming too comfortable. The seed of unfriendliness is becoming unapproachable. The seed of a downfall is pride. If something in your life isn't growing, consider what it is that you planted.

Day Twenty-Three: You don't need permission to participate in your own life.

Day Twenty-Four: Be open to the possibility that you may have read a situation wrong. Be open to feedback that helps you grow. Be open to try again. Be open to asking for help. Be open to being responsible for you. Your world changes when you are open.

Day Twenty-Five: Note to self: Stop overlooking the benefits of a great nap! You can't run on an empty tank.

Day Twenty-Six: Surround yourself with positive people. Smile. Speak kindly. Stop gossiping. Encourage someone. Serve others. Start a new hobby. Take a class. Go on an adventure. Make an overdue apology. Focus on being a better you. Do these things and trust me, whatever it is that is attempting to keep you stuck will lose its significance in your life and you will be moving once again.

Day Twenty-Seven: You have the right to say no without explanation.

Day Twenty-Eight: Love conquers a multitude of almost everything except a dirty diaper! You can't love that away, it must be changed immediately! Seriously, take each day and live in the moment. You might not always get it right but being present in their lives is a gift for both you and your child.

Day Twenty-Nine: One small stone thrown into the river can change its flow. You can be the stone. You can change the flow. Don't wait for others, do it yourself. You possess what the world needs. Create the ripple and other stones will follow.

Day Thirty: Decide to let go of things that are toxic and unproductive for your journey.

CHAPTER 8

Borrowed Jewels

Along the way, I have encountered some wonderful people who pour into my life just as much as I've poured into their lives. With their permission, I am sharing some of what I've learned from them over the years. It is my prayer that they touch you as well.

What is one piece of advice that you would give to a new parent?

Enjoy every moment as the time goes by so fast! Also, there is no textbook to this: it's a journey that you continue to learn and grow each day. – Danielle Tolbert

Start saving for college now and don't parent out of fear. – Nichole Turner

Take tons and tons of pictures because the time goes so fast and they change in an instant. - Tylaine Parker

No baby ever cried themselves to death! Having two babies that screamed for one year straight had me frazzled but someone told me that once – and one night I let my daughter cry. The next night she cried for five minutes and then went to sleep. – Jennifer Lash Lewis

Being a parent doesn't come with a manual. We all made mistakes. Just love them and grow in love. With every year there is a new person evolving. Enjoy the moments good and bad. – Shawn Shelton Pierce

Enjoy each and every moment. Don't ever get too busy to enjoy their childhood. They grow up very quickly and you never want to look back and say "I wish I would have spent more time with them." – Helena Porter

Let love lead you. Enjoy every new discovery your baby makes. Learn from them as they learn from you. – Patricia Eastland

Keep a journal to document the journey. Give it to them when they become parents. – Sarita Brooker

Put the Super Parent cape away. It's overrated. Accept help when offered and pay it forward later. Kiss and love your babies without hesitation - they'll repay those kisses when they're old enough to realize you really do give unconditional love. – Diana Potter Crawford

Train up a child in the way he should go. Second, leave an inheritance for your children's children. – Marcia Church Lynch

Never be too busy to hug your child. Instant comfort for you both. – Deidre Thompson

Some days you can plan all you want but nothing will go as expected....it's totally fine to live in the moment! – Niya Hargreaves

Shower your child with light and love. The world needs more happiness and love! It is the best way to repay God for this immeasurable blessing. – Kristen Stanton

Grandparent wisdom is some of the funniest yet most profound pieces of advice you will ever receive. What was one piece of advice your grandparents shared that you've never forgotten?

Always be sure to have on clean underwear! You never know when you'll be in an accident and end up in the ER!! – Shawn Shelton Pierce

My great grandmother said "think before you speak." My grandmother said "God bless the child that's got his own." – Michele Kelly

A good lathering of lotion will cure anything. – Daphne Evans

Pay your rent first. You can always get a meal. – Vicki D. Sanders

Leave it at the altar. – Deidre Thompson

To have a successful marriage, we need to pray together and trust in the Lord. – Ron Reinert

Never give up. You must persevere! – James Eastland (this was actually advice that my grandmother gave to my father, her son.)

Always put some of your money in savings. She took me to Beneficial Bank to open up my first account. – Autumn Redcross

One piece of advice I wish someone would've given me when I was younger is_____.

In life you will have many obstacles but always remember that it is not how you start, it is how you finish. - George Reid, Jr.

You are enough because God says so. You cannot please everyone and that is okay! – Nichole Turner

Let my voice be the loudest one in my head. – Tangela Harden

If it is not your passion, don't say yes to something simply because you don't want to disappoint someone. – Yvette D. Styer

Your heart will be broken a few times but don't let that stop you from being open to love. – Yvette D. Styer

Learn how to play the stock market. – Robin Jenkins Whitley

Work to live, don't live to work. – Robin Jenkins Whitley

If you must be a fool, be a fool on your own terms. – Charles "Cheeba" Davis

How you treat folks is not necessarily how they'll treat you. – Chariesse Eastland

Create and protect your relationship with the Savior. It will keep your mind, your heart, and your very soul. – Nikki Stanley

Actions show a person's heart more than their words. – Kimberly V. Jones

You are not obligated to save everyone and sacrifice your life for other people. Live your life. They are grown and can take care of themselves. – JeNell LaRue

You can't make everybody happy. If I had listened to that, I would not have tried so hard to be a people pleaser. It took me some time, but I finally got over that! – Patricia Eastland

Time will come and go. It will not wait for you. – Charlene Cruz

Do not allow yourself to be so paralyzed with fear that you don't even try. Even if you try and don't succeed, there's a lesson learned which is better than looking back with regrets. – Erica Bantom Martin

CHAPTER 9

Your turn!

This chapter is dedicated to you! It is an opportunity to record your thoughts.

Danette M. Reid

Dream Big! What has God told you that He will do in your life? What steps are you taking to prepare for the gift? What do you need to let go of in order to receive it?

Describe a few lessons that you've learned over the past few years that have been life changing.

If you are feeling stuck, use any of the following prompts below to organize your thoughts:

1. What are you holding onto that is not allowing you to experience God's peace?

2. In order to find peace, I need to......

3. Lately, I have been struggling with.......

Use the space below to recall an adverse situation that you now realize was necessary for your journey.

Who are your treasured friends? List and write a favorite memory that you've shared with each one. Then do yourself a favor and send them a note of thanks for being a true friend.

For the next seven days, use the space below to record at least one thing for which you are grateful!

Take the Word and hide it in your Heart! Use the space below to record a few of your favorite scripture passages. When you need to be encouraged, refer to this page for easy reference.

CHAPTER 10

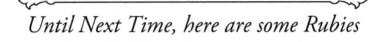

Until Next Time, here are some Rubies that I'd like to leave you with....

Δ *The power of silence should never be underestimated. Every comment does not require a response.*

Δ *Blaming others for things that are within your control means that either (1) you are in denial about the part you played in the outcome or (2) you have given another person way too much power over your life...only you can identify which option applies to you. Either way, it may be time to look in the mirror.*

Δ *The easy thing to do in not always the right thing to do. The choice belongs to you but consider this: Easy but wrong normally comes back to you and you'll end up doing what's right in the end. Do yourself a favor, just do the right thing ☺*

Δ *Growth comes when one accepts that although they may be doing the best that they can with the tools that they have, that the time has come to acquire new tools.*

Δ*Time, attention, and encouragement can help change the direction of any child's life. Actually, it works for adults too!*

Δ *Authentic living is a freedom that you will only gain when you learn to love the real you!*

Δ *Today is a day unlike any other. It is filled with new grace and mercy. The things of this day are already predestined for God knew about it before you were placed in your mother's womb. Trust Him and go with the flow because He has you in His hands.*

Δ *When you walk in your purpose, even the detours along the way will work for your good.*

Δ *Love moves at its own pace. If you try to rush it, you are almost guaranteed to get in its way.*

Δ *It is better to walk in your own purpose than to crawl through someone else's. If it is not yours, do not try to own it.*

Δ *Kindness is a way to let the light of God shine through you. It costs you nothing but is worth its weight in God to the one who receives the kindness that you extend.*

Every time I put my pen to paper, a story is born and an experience is shared. I am grateful for you, my readers, whom God has purposed to come along for the ride.

He has something in store for your life. Your journey starts today. Follow Him boldly and with all of your heart and know that He will neither leave nor forsake you. My prayer for you is found in Rom. 15:13 - *May the God of hope fill you with all joy and peace as you trust in him, so that you may overflow with hope by the power of the Holy Spirit.* Until next time, God bless and keep you will be among my prayers.

Danette M. Reid is an encourager. Her first book, "Jewels from the Journey... Lessons from the Life of an Ordinary Woman Serving an Extraordinary God was released in August, 2009. *Jewels Too...The Journey Continues* is her second book. She is currently working on her third book: A Collection of Rubies...Jewels for our young people.

To connect with Danette, please contact her via email at danettereidthewriter@gmail.com.

Printed in the United States
By Bookmasters